Tamia T. Scott

MeMaw's Garden

Written by Tyonie Patterson

Illustrated by Nyisha Gabourel

This book belongs to:

"Tamia, here is 1 juicy red tomato."

"MeMaw, here are 2 crunchy green apples. Biting into them is a hassle."

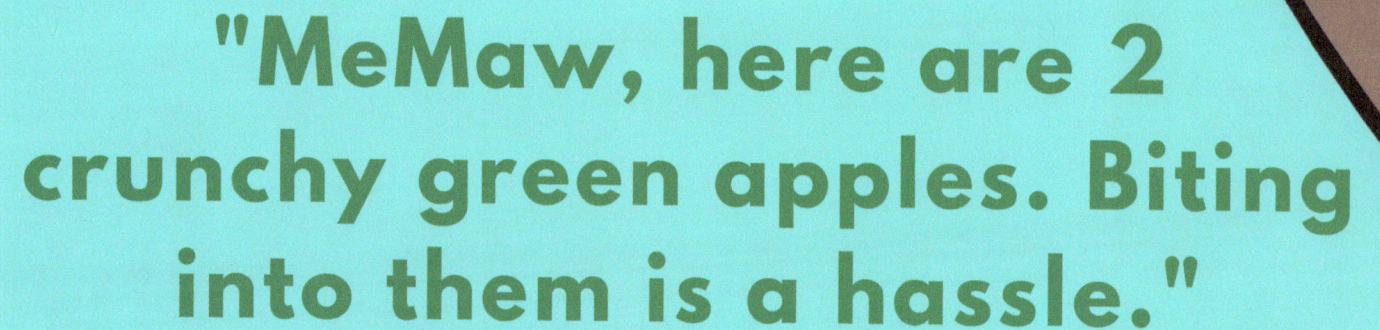

"Tamia, here are 3 raw orange carrots. Let's feed some to the parrots."

"MeMaw, here are 4 sweet red strawberries. They are the same color as cherries."

"MeMaw, here are 6 mushy purple grapes. Let's eat them during our break."

"Tamia, here are 7

starchy brown potatoes."

"MeMaw, here are 8 tart red cherries. They are small like raspberries."

"Tamia, here are 9 bitter green bell peppers. Let's cut them together."

"MeMaw, here are 10 sour yellow lemons. Let's take some to our neighbor, Ms. Simmons."

Questions

1. Which food items did MeMaw share?

2. Which food items did Tamia share?

3. What is your favorite fruit and vegetable?

4. Why should we eat fruits and vegetables ?

About the Author

Tyonie Patterson is the author of the Tamia T. Scott Series. She was born and raised in Los Angeles, California. Tyonie is a proud alumni of Prairie View A&M University and Hampton University. Her passion is developing children's speech and language skills, especially with literacy activities. Tyonie created this series as a resource for parents, educators, and organizations which will allow them to teach their children basic concepts (e.g., counting, colors, prepositions, vocabulary, etc.). Additionally, Tyonie created this series to celebrate African Americans as the main character. Only 12% of children's books feature African Americans as main characters, and the percentage is lower for other minority groups. She believes we must diversify our bookshelves because it can give our children a sense of connectivity, relatability, and self-value.

About the Tamia T. Scott Series

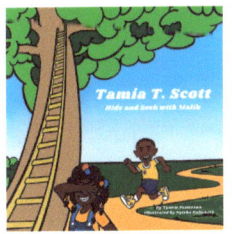

The Tamia T. Scott Series teaches children basic concepts such as colors, counting, and vocabulary. It's an interactive story that families can apply to their daily lives (e.g., from talking about fruits and vegetables to playing hide and seek outside, etc.). Most importantly, the Tamia T. Scott Series is a representation of beautiful black children across the world. REPRESENTATION MATTERS !

www.tamiatscottseries.com

www.ingramcontent.com/pod-product-compliance
Lightning Source LLC
Chambersburg PA
CBHW041201290426
44109CB00002B/98